Born in Exeter in 1968, Melanie  English and drama lecturer, an ... full-time carer.

Since taking up spoken word in ... she has performed at WOMAD ... the Edinburgh Fringe and poetry ... .. country, including multiple feature sets for t ... ...e Bar and Hammer & Tongue.

She is also an established page poet, widely published in journals. A collection of her page poetry, *My Cloth-Eared Heart*, was published by Oversteps in 2017.

Can You See Where I'm Coming From?

Melanie Branton

Burning Eye

BurningEyeBooks
Never Knowingly
Mainstream

This edition published by Burning Eye Books 2018

www.burningeye.co.uk

@burningeyebooks

Burning Eye Books
15 West Hill, Portishead, BS20 6LG

ISBN 978-1-911570-56-1

Printed & bound by ImprintDigital.com, UK

Can You See Where I'm Coming From?

In memory of my parents,
John (1928–2015) and Olive (1928–2013).

Also, for Robert, who's been a thoroughly nice chap.

CONTENTS

DNA

DNA

I'm proud of the fact I'm Cornish.
I'm proud that, of all the flags, of all the nations,
ours is the cheapest to photocopy.
The standard of St Piran.
See? Even our patron saint
has got a better name than yours.
George? Patrick? David? Andrew?
They all sound like guys who work
at the ICT helpdesk,
but you can't imagine Piran ever asking anyone,
'Have you tried switching it off and on again?'

I'm proud of the fact I'm Cornish.
It's why my skin goes red and burnt on a hot day:
because even when I'm sunbathing
I can't quite bring myself to put the cream on first.

I'm proud of the fact I'm Cornish.
I'm at the head of an unstoppable army,
mounted on a white horse,
possibly wearing a tricorn,
marching on Westminster,
demanding we be declared
an autonomous enclave,
taking back control of the Tamar.

I am King Arthur, returned to save his people
when they need him most!
I am the Lady of the Lake!

My ancestors were shamanic druids,
appearing out of the mist,
looking a bit like Gandalf,
or photogenic smugglers
dressed like New Romantics,
in frilly shirts and knee breeches.
I might not have a personality,

but I've got an identity.
I'm not like everyone else.

Behind this façade of a shy, mild-mannered,
gawky, middle-aged frump
with no discernible achievements whatsoever
lies a rakish daredevil,
a swashbuckling rebel, performing deeds of derring-do,
cocking a snook in the face of authority.
Appearances are deceptive. They must be.
You can't argue with blood.

But poke too hard at the genealogy
and I actually find generations of
subsistence farmers, scratching a poor living
from Atlantic-scoured slopes,
marrying their first cousins
to keep a handkerchief of land in the family,
the kind of men who blow their own brains out
in unrefurbished kitchens with no mains electricity
because the milk price has dropped again.

My DNA is as brittle, cheap and unwholesome
as a barley sugar twist.
We're stuck out on a promontory
miles away from anywhere. Marooned.
They didn't choose this place.
They'd have shot off to London,
where the money is, if they'd had the chance.

When I meet my Cornish relatives
once every twenty years or so
at weddings and funerals
we have nothing to say to each other.
They're too busy keeping the rusting tractor of life on the road
to be the pirates I want them to be

and I have all the ardent Cornish nationalism
of someone with one vaguely Cornish grandparent,
of someone actually born in the Other County
(the one beginning with 'D'. Ssh!).
I'm like one of these Irish Americans.
I've only been to Cornwall once.

CASTLES

I'm at a workshop at a poetry festival
and we're supposed to be writing down our thoughts,
but the only thoughts in my mind right now
are how the knob of butter in a baked potato
looks a bit like a vagina, and how I spoke too quietly
when the featured poet asked my name
and now he's signed my book, 'To Melamine',

and there's a little boy here – his dad's got a hipster beard,
his mum's carrying the *Guardian* and wearing lots of
artisan-crafted jewellery. He's called Alfred
or Arthur or Horatio, or one of those names,
he's not been backwards about coming forwards all session
and when we're asked who would like to share their work,
he strides towards the microphone as if it were his birthright.

And I know it's shameful that I'm angry at his 'cockiness',
I know that rosebuds should not be kept tightly shut,
they should be allowed to bloom,
but I'm broken that he assumes by six
what my father could not believe by eighty-six:
that his voice is entitled to be heard.

My father thought that poems had to rhyme. It was the rule.
He liked the kind of poem that gets sneered at
at your open-mics and he would have hated this poem.
He was very quiet.
So, sneer if you like, but know his life
was measured out in rigid metre,
a regular pattern that he could not break, like a-b-a-b,
like bricks cemented in English bond, a pattern of cheap jeans,
of chequered shirts from Millets,
of sandwiches wrapped in greaseproof paper,
of wheelbarrows and hods, of scaffolding poles
and cycle rides home and Swarfega,
of weekly manila pay packets
with very little in them, then allotments and the dole.

His syntax was twisted to fit the scheme
someone else had chosen,
he was stuck in a place that didn't suit him,
like a forced rhyme. In shit jobs,
initiative isn't welcome – you do what you're told –
and you, with your book clubs
and your networking events, and your therapists
and your artistic free expression workshops
for fucking toddlers, will never understand
how scared he was, every single second
of his eighty-six years, of saying the wrong thing.

We have no castles, we have no historic names,
we have no family crests, we have no ancestral lands.
We have no mangoes, no cardamom pods,
no plantains, no patois.
We have nothing
that people with hipster beards
and artisan-crafted jewellery
will pay ten quid to culturally appropriate.
We have only battered bus shelters,
scuffed melamine tabletops,
miles and miles of blank, unending, broken pavements.

And people with hipster beards and artisan-crafted jewellery
will only ever pay ten quid
to see us battered and blank and broken
and being very quiet.

THE RESPECTABLES

My uncles left school at fourteen, but winged it
into white collars, made themselves
semi-detached. We had to take
our shoes off when we went round.

Shamed by our filthy carpets,
our low ceilings,
my parents never let us forget
we were (not 'was'!) better than our neighbours.
We had the West Country scolded
out of us, made cognisant
of minute distinctions of grammar.
We had less money, fewer possessions,
less hope, fewer prospects,
but at least we knew the difference.

THIS ISN'T WHAT I SIGNED UP FOR!

Space Dust and Spangles.
Corona pop, Cobana, Texan, Montego.
The brand names were faraway, shiny,
Golden Wonder the market leader in crisps
(Walkers were pedestrian).

Gary Glitter was on *Top of the Pops*
in a silver jumpsuit and one day
the whole school got taken out of lessons
to watch something on the wheelie telly:
Concorde was breaking the sound barrier
and, well, we didn't yet know what barriers
Gary was breaking, but it felt like the future
was preparing for landing. The tyres hadn't yet burst.

'Supersonic' became the word of the moment.
Nobody knew what it meant –
'Wow, Tracey, your shoes are supersonic!' –
but its actual dictionary definition wasn't the point.
The laws of physics were being rewritten
and now our ambitions stretched out along endless corridors
like the *Magpie* appeal, our dreams as bouffant
as Mick Robertson's hair.

I wanted to be an astronaut.
When they showed us about the Space Shuttle
on the schools' programmes, it sounded a realistic career path.
The Moon was going to be Earth's dormitory overflow town –
a kind of supra-atmospheric Bradley Stoke. They said
astronauts ate dehydrated food and I pictured them in their
space suits bending over a Baby Belling, stirring a Vesta curry.

In the future everything would be dried or frozen
and I knew this, because I watched *Tomorrow's World*.
They promised us holograms and jet packs,
but couldn't predict mobile phones and duvets.
They had vision.

Most adults didn't. They smoked at work
and drove drunk without a seatbelt,
but were scared of microwaves and tampons.
My mother scowled in the power cuts,
not feeling the thrill of reading *Jinty* by candlelight.

When I lay in bed at night, my top sheet tucked tightly in,
I was hurtling through the cosmos in a space capsule.
The thought made me tingle, like Space Dust and Spangles.

OUR END OF TOWN

Tight-lipped poverty,
faces grimly set, as we bit down
on our want.
Never complain.
Never admit.

Things that weren't talked about:
howling and grunting that was muffled,
bruises that weren't explained.

Like cats, we had our territory.
Where middle-class people saw friendliness,
we saw encroachment.
There was a brutal courtesy
in keeping out of others' space:
the omerta of low income.

The worst of sins:
showing off. Standing out,
not blending in. Blowing your own trumpet.
'Think you're really somebody, don't you?'
That most cutting of rejoinders.
The aspiration was to be nobody, to be invisible,
to disappear. Our faces grey and puffy
as pilling overwashed Y-fronts,
we sought camouflage in all that concrete.

Net curtains.
Best clothes put on for the doctor's.
Seats given up for our elders.
Thank you, driver.
Curt nods from the opposite pavement.
Undergoing our very own Great Vowel Shift
every time we answered the telephone

Tea on the table at 5.15
for when Dad cycled back from the site.

Sunday's roast, carved carefully,
lasted until Thursday.
Bulked out with stuffing,
it became greyer and harder,
shrank like an atrophied muscle.
We fumbled and circulated it in our mouths
as though performing a blowjob
under coercion: kept up the fear-stoked pretence
that we liked it, unable to suppress
the shudder as we swallowed.

And when we dreamed it was
unambitiously in puce- and mustard-coloured
telly that hurt your ears. The blazered host
with a Lancashire accent and Hollywood teeth,
his smut uniquely indulged,
offering modest cash prizes in gold envelopes,
a car on a creaky revolve, surrounded by footlights.

COMMUNICATION SKILLS

My father left notes
on cut-up pieces of cardboard;
Mr Kipling and Mr Kellogg
were his secretaries.
He formed rune-like letters
with a stubby pencil
that he'd sharpened with a Swiss Army knife –
the same one he used to cut his nails.

A year on, I still find them where he filed them
between the pages of flicked-through books,
in the pockets of coats I forgot to take to Oxfam,
at the bottom of the cutlery drawer –
records of vegetables planted that year,
lottery numbers,
dimensions measured in feet and inches,
the twenty-eight member states of the EU.

He wrote things down
to try to put things in order,
to try to make sense of things that had happened.
I comprehend the enormousness of his absence
by breaking it into verse lines.

THE BOX

My mother lived inside an eighteen-inch box
in our front room,
with Terry and June, the Goodies
and the Six Million Dollar Man.
She was a woman barely alive.
Gentlemen, we couldn't rebuild her.
We didn't have the technology.
Nothing we could say or do
could ever be as funky as that gibbon.

She came out now and then, of course,
to cook the dinner and to do the ironing,
but she never really looked at us,
always had this twitchy restlessness.
She couldn't wait to get back and open up another
can of laughter, speed her life up
to Steve Austin's pace, overtaking in slow motion.

We weren't to disturb her viewing,
afraid to move, to speak, to breathe.
Judge it wrong and the jellyfish sting
of her hand against my thigh
left sudden, scarlet marks across my heart.

It wasn't that she never tried to wean herself off that teat.
She was always on the look-out for novelties –
anything to break the tedium of housework.
When I was nine, she had a fad for baking bread.
The table juddered as she thumped the dough,
her angry fingers choking the gluey mass,
murdering its amorphousness.
She took a couple of courses at the tech,
so proud of her French and German GCSEs,
fourteen when the Blitz bombed her out of school.

It never lasted, though. It never led to anything.
She couldn't really see how it could.

The careers advice we got at school
bemused her. 'Find a job you can be happy in?
But you're not supposed to be happy at work.
If you were, they wouldn't have to pay you.'
Like everybody who's never had any,
the only thing she understood was money.

She didn't know what she wanted,
claimed she was content
with marriage to a meek and scarcely visible man
who kept very, very, very quiet and did what he was told,
handed her his pay packet every Friday
like a shy child giving Mummy
the finger painting he'd done at nursery.
She did all the things that frightened him,
like reading and writing and speaking,
paying the bills, interceding with those in authority.
At night, they hid together
under a balding candlewick bedspread.
The rest of the time, he cocooned himself in silence
and she climbed back into her box.

She craved something better for us,
but even her aspirations were made-for-TV:
blurred clichés clipped from *Crown Court*, *General Hospital*,
To the Manor Born. A job she thought
wouldn't require 'connections',
that you could get just by passing exams,
and that would transubstantiate us into the kind of people
she distrusted, despised and feared, but worshipped.
The kind of people who cooked with garlic and drank wine
and had dinner parties and listened to classical music
and went on holiday on planes.
She'd never be able to talk to us –
I mean really talk to us – again, of course.
It would be like sending us on a one-way mission to Mars,
but she was prepared to make that sacrifice,

because Mars was a better place.
Happiness could not be found
anywhere on Earth, but happiness must surely
be found in that strange, red, radioactive world
the other side of the asteroids.

Times changed. *Celebrity Squares*
and *Sale of the Century* gave way to *Strike It Lucky*,
but she never did. The glamour, the excitement,
that indefinable something she hoped would be transferred
down the cathode ray tube never reached her screen.

I got out, fed up of having to compete and losing to
shadow puppets, Borrowers,
little cuckoos wearing too much pan make-up
who abseiled into my home and her heart down the aerial
like the Milk Tray Man.

I wish I'd tried harder.
My mother now lives inside a five-foot box.
I'll never be able to get her out of that one.

DARKNESS

the colour the day goes
when it's been left too long in the toaster
when the light's all vanished up the hoover
and all that's left is the black carpet
bruised banana liquorice bootlace
freshly laid tarmac
a vinyl album spinning on a turntable
at 365 revolutions per year

DRINKING IT BLACK

My sister's wedding could easily have been a diplomatic incident.
All celebration had to breathe in
to squeeze itself into my parents' size-6 budget.
They cut their coat according to their meagre cloth
and if she, or, even worse, her in-laws, had contributed
anything more than the haberdashery,
my parents would have been shamed.

She resigned herself and did the best she could,
made the bridesmaids' dresses from strawberry-coloured acetate
that did look very much like taffeta in a dim light.
True, the rugby club with its Marmite-coloured walls
and the stage with its multicoloured Bacofoil curtain
wasn't quite the ambience she had in mind,
but they got hired caterers in for the wedding breakfast
and it was only the evening finger buffet we had to put together
in my mother's kitchen. I was dispatched to Tesco
for another tub of cream cheese to fill the vol-au-vents,
while my mum shaved slivers off the wafer-thin smoked salmon
to make it go further.

At the top table, my father in his new suit
looked as if he'd been ironed,
manacled in his unfamiliar buttoned collar and cuffs.
The waitress brought him black coffee by mistake
and he was too shy to correct her.
Even though he was the one paying her,
even though he was the customer
who is always right,
he knew in his soul he was always wrong.
He forced down the dark, bitter drink
in hunched, staccato sips
and when I offered to call her back
and ask for a jug of milk,
he insisted he really did drink it that way sometimes.

He'd been adamant he didn't need help with his speech,

made a list of notes in his diary,
but when he stood up to speak
his face blancmanged. Like a searchlight,
the eyes of the room found him out and exposed him.
Freezing under their beam, he managed to stutter out,
'I would like to welcome you…' His voice became strangled,
hoarse, tailed off. The eyes glanced at each other.
There was shifting, coughing. Time was suspended.
He stood there, silent, white and rigid, crucified,
the Hanging Man. I gripped my napkin and stared at my lap.
At the back of the room, someone stifled a giggle.
The best man looked at the groom,
the groom looked at the bride. She fingered the lace of her dress.
Expectant smiles solidified.
A couple of the cousins whispered to each other.
He concertinaed back onto his chair,
all the air squeezed out of him.

Breathing again, the room broke into applause,
some cheers. No one cared.
Less time to wait for the toast and the cake.
But my father shrank inside himself,
his face scalded with shame.

The in-laws drove us home later that night
to save us getting a cab.
My father said nothing.
My mother talked too much;
her overbright, overloud, clanging bell of a voice
hurt my ears. I stared out of the window
as if she was somebody else's mother,
a colleague from another department, a stranger on a bus.
The siren of a passing ambulance
crowed three times and I wanted to weep.

FACELESS

There was a   gap in the family photo album
where my   grandfather should have been,
a   pause in the conversation, followed by
a swift   changing of subjects,
a being sent to my room.
Explanations, when unavoidable,
took the form of   further negatives:
'He had an accident. After that,
he was never   quite himself.'

Though   absent without leave,
he was ever present in my father's
flinching retreat at the first sign of confrontation,
his cobweb sense of   self, his night terrors,
my mother's shielding him from any knocks,
her wild insistence, 'He mustn't be upset!'
but I never saw his   face.

Years later, I was e-mailed a   photo
by a distant cousin in Canada.
He wears his   cap pulled well down,
as if already hiding from schemes and spies.
I can just make out he has my father's   jaw,
but he remains as   faceless here
as the   body they pulled from Topsham Lock
after three days putrefying in the water.
They identified him by his hair
and the asylum labels in his clothes.

NANA

Born within the sound of Bow bells,
never lost the taste for Cockney street food,
jellied eels, vinegared cockles and mussels, pigs' trotters,
never forgot the taste of poverty,
reused wrapping paper until it felt like suede,
saved up old soap scraps and sewed them into a sponge mitt,

loved Marx almost as much as Jesus,
sometimes got confused as to which said,
'Woe unto you that are rich,
for ye have received your consolation,'
and which, 'Workers of the world unite,
you have nothing to lose but your chains,'
bought me a Bible with her Green Shield stamps
and then marked with a cross a passage in Luke
she said proved God agreed with her
about the right way of doing the washing-up,
gave us nightmares with her own parables,
The Boy Who Accidentally Gouged His Own Eyes Out
When Carelessly Opening a Parcel,
The Man Who Lost an Arm to Septicaemia
After Catching It on a Needle Left in the Wallpaper,
a mind as stiff and immoveable as the clasp
on her enormous black handbag,

went to France in the First World War,
took Jesus with her, whether He wanted to go or not,
won a medal for her voluntary work there,
came back with a Tommy husband from Halwill,
found rural Devon more foreign than France,
loved the French,
never learnt French,
thought you just had to shout loud enough in English,
but made friends for life, was regularly invited back to Calais
to gesture and shout incomprehensibly,

wore her dead son on a chain round her neck,
kept her dead brothers on the mantelpiece,
kept her dead husband's guard's whistle,
never forgot the name of the railway wagon was Capitalism,
the wagon that backed into him and poisoned him with the piss
from his own crushed kidneys,
all the railway gave her was the whistle,
was still fighting both world wars singlehanded,

gave extravagantly to the Lifeboats in memory of her son,
retrospectively funding the lifeboat that hadn't been there,
left her body to medical research,
an old soap scrap she couldn't bear see go to waste.

SECRET PASSAGES

Do you want to be in my gang?
I'm the Secret One, the Famous One,
the One Finder Out and Cat.
I'm looking for mysteries to solve.
I'm looking for clues.

When I was nine, my reading age
was a shadow twice my height:
like they said in the primary school reading test,
beguiling idiosyncrasy tyrannical somnambulist
ineradicable belligerent fictitious enigma.
I spent my nights with a torch under the bedclothes
when I was supposed to be asleep,
looking for secret passages to somewhere else.
I wanted my life to be scripted by Enid Blyton.

Life was full of small mysteries.
Why had my parents sold their car
and stopped having bacon and eggs
for breakfast on a Sunday?
When I asked my mum if I could go horseriding
or tapdancing, like the other kids in my class,
why did she look in her purse,
then say, 'Don't be silly.
A clumsy lump like you –
you'd look ridiculous on a horse'?
Why did my friend's mum turn up in tears
on our doorstep one morning?
When the dad came round ten minutes later,
my parents wouldn't let him in.
(The answer to that one turned out to be simple.
My mum told us: she'd fallen over
and scraped her knee.)

In Enid Blyton, the children didn't just have bedrooms –
they had a nursery, as well, but we didn't.
What was that all about?

They spoke with authority to shopkeepers
and policemen, told them what to do,
went anywhere they liked.
I'd never have been allowed to get away with that.
Why didn't their parents give them a clip round the ear?

I did find some members to join my gang:
my sister, a girl in my class at school
and the old man who lived next door,
but the trouble with having a member
in the early stages of dementia
was he kept forgetting the secret passwords
and, in the end, making up secret passwords
was all we had to do.
There was a disappointing lack of shifty-looking men
with bushy beards hanging around our street.
It was more like *Scooby-Doo*:
the villains were people you actually knew
hiding behind a mask.
I didn't have a clue.

I never did find a secret passage.
Turned out there was no panelling to tap
beneath the woodchip wallpaper
in a three-bedroom terraced house,
Mellow Bird's with Mr Kipling
wasn't what they meant by Kaffee und Kuchen
and it was no good looking for Narnia
at the back of an MDF wardrobe.
I'd got it all wrong.
Like they said in the primary school reading test,
grotesque susceptible slovenly gnome.

It was my reading age, not me,
that slipped away at night to other centuries,
was a Traveller in Time, made a Journey
to the Centre of the Earth, blagged its way
through the gates of Troy in a wooden horse.

EDUCATION

BAGGAGE

The suitcase packed for boarding school
was a hard bargain struck
with a Puritan God.
You could take fun with you –
hardback books,
your patchwork quilt,
the battery-powered radio cassette –
but it was going to cost.
You prayed you wouldn't have to change trains at Bristol,
but, God, of course, had other ideas.
Then, worst of all, the Underground at Paddington,
your arm pulled half out of its socket
as you heaved your rectangular red vinyl albatross
up over the steps.
Your palm stung like Jesus's and
you had a beaded line imprinted on it
for days after.

More and more, I opted for asceticism.
Sod the patchwork quilt.
Scratchy regulation school blankets would do.
The radio cassette? Forget it – I'd sing
or carry memories of chart hits in my head.
You'd think my pleasure-hating deity would approve,
but, no, he was, it seems, conspiring with my mum
to punish me, even when I gave up fun.
As I headed for the door,
bearably slimline case in hand,
she'd hand me a bag of 'treats' –
cans of Coke, paving-stone-sized chocolate bars,
tins of frigging tuna.

Is this what all mothers do?
Send their children out into the world
handicapped like a racehorse,
weighed down by a love they do not want?

FAT

I'll tell you something, and I'll tell you flat:
when I was a child, I was very fat.
I had fat fingers, I had fat thumbs,
fat feet, fat calves, fat thighs, fat bum,

fat chest, fat belly, fat hips, fat waist,
fat chin, fat cheeks, fat ears, fat face,
fat shoulders, fat elbows, fat wrists, fat hands,
fat liver, fat lungs, fat heart, fat glands.

In case it's not clear, my friends, the issue
was an overabundance of adipose tissue
and everyone thought I was a stupid twat,
as I was very shy and I was very fat.

My clothes didn't fit, I was so fat:
tight vest, tight pants, tight coat, tight hat,
tight socks, tight trousers, tight jumper, tight shirt,
tight slip, tight tights, tight dress, tight skirt.

And when my classmates talked, as classmates do,
of who'd end up paired off with who,
they didn't pussyfoot about:
'No boy will ever ask you out!
You'll never be Mrs – always Miss!
You're much too overweight to kiss!'

Then I dreamed a hot boy would come along
and prove that all they said was wrong,
but the chance of my attracting him
was the one thing about me that was very slim.

Slim chance, slim hopes of avoiding a kicking,
slim faith, slim luck, slim dreams, slim pickings.
No glitz, no glamour, no fashions, no trends,
no fun, no love, no life, no friends.

Fat ankles, fat knees, fat heels, fat toes,
fat neck, fat jaw, fat head, fat nose,
fat breasts, fat cunt, fat knuckles, fat palms,
fat back, fat front, fat legs, fat arms,

fat, fat, fat, fat, fat, fat, fat, fat,
fat, fat, fat, fat, fat, fat, fat, fat.

RESULTS

Lines have been drawn
in red on the list on the classroom wall. It is rank
order: distinctions at the top, failures
at the bottom, the mediocre in between. Everyone
has a number and lines have been drawn,
at 50%, 75%, quarantining the cleverer names from
infection by the thick. We jostle round to gawp and point,
bitch at the spews, take the piss out of the durrs,
taking our stand. Defensive.

Our private humiliations have been flourished
like the ninety-five theses. This house believes
competition is healthy, like ice-cold baths,
unmediated feral bully-offs
on the sports pitch, cross-country runs
in the rain. Social mobility will never be achieved
without toughness, a good old scrap.
Work out your own salvation: it's each girl for herself.

I was the right side of the line, but still wrong
for my mother. 'Second place is not
too bad, I suppose, but try to come first next time.'

I never did. I have crept into a tentative adulthood,
trusting no one, introspective as Hamlet,
lost away from Wittenberg in a world where
routes to power snake more subtly
than academic league tables, classroom workings-out.
They poured their poison into my ear and I became petrified,
needing to be judged, inclined to draw red lines on myself.

My therapist charges me with all-or-nothing thinking.
'Human beings,' she says,
'cannot be reduced to just "the best" or "rubbish". Be less hard
on yourself.' But I am not hard, I am soft, and it is too late:
the thought has been impressed on me, like a red biro
pressed down on cheap paper. This is how I score myself.
I can do no other. God help me.

LOVE WAS THE DRUG

When I was twelve, I dated Adam Ant,
but then I dumped him for Simon Le Bon.
I also had a thing with Julian Cope
simultaneously going on.

I flirted with Nick Rhodes, as well,
and (this is a shameful admission)
I had a fling with Johnny Logan
just after Eurovision.

It was the best time to be a teenage girl
and this is the thing that clinches:
you could buy a new boyfriend every week
(though all of them were seven inches).

Didn't know how to talk to boys?
Had no social skills? Couldn't mingle?
Didn't matter, 'cause the charts were always filled
with eligible singles.

They were dressed in leather trousers
and shirts with flounces, too.
They'd done their hair and makeup
to look pretty, just for you.

You pinned them down on that revolving table,
you felt like a love goddess, you felt like Venus.
When you plunged that needle down,
the hit was intravenous.

Love was the drug
and the music was the drug
and your body was the drug
and your youth was the drug
and the rhythm was the drug
and the bassline was the drug
and the drug was in your blood!

That rhythm had you hypnotised,
like a mesmeriser.
They'd synthesised synthetic highs
on their synthesiser.

I could be Top of the Pops
in my fantasies, girl.
I could get a Whole Lotta Love
just by touching my Yellow Pearl.

I was Queen of the Universe
and everything in it!
The whole world revolved around me
at forty-five revolutions per minute.

BUILDING THE READER
AS IDEAL CONSUMER

I thought Martini was as sophisticated
as it looked on the adverts,
but she gave a little cough and said, with manners
that matched her Private Girls' Day School Trust voice,
'I shan't put this out on the wine table.
I expect you've brought it because you'd like to drink it
yourself.'

I nodded gratefully, then all night smiled and danced
at the margins of the party. Since then I've learned not to trust
those telly-suave men in dinner jackets,
ladies in velvet dresses the colour of my shame.

CIDER

I'd rather drink cider than soda,
though cider, alas, makes me sadder.
I'm sadder, but wiser,
when sozzled on cider,
but I'm often sold soda
by a pseudo-crusader
who never drinks alcohol – someone forbade her –
she won't have one soupcon of cider inside her.

She's truly teetotal,
not teetering on it,
she tuts when I try to drink tots,
gets totally tetchy, it gets on her tits,
though the tots that I toss back are truly quite titchy.

She does make me shudder.
Well, 'Sod her!' I say.
'I'd rather drink cider, any old day!'

(I'll just add one coda –
I'll sometimes drink soda,
more often than Spider-Man
test-drives a Skoda.
I have to concede, soda's not odious.
Soda and I are on terms quite harmonious,

but I'll add one more rider –
I'd rather drink cider.
It's a stimulant beverage
and that's the decider,
and so I consider it
sweeter than soda.
Though it just doesn't suit her,
it surely suits me.
I'd rather drink cider than soda, you see.)

I'd rather drink vino than Vimto

and I vow to you that's not bravado:
I vacuum up vats of it,
venerate venues
with Chardonnay, Shiraz and Veuve
on their menus.

I'm vaguely enthralled
by its velvety voodoo
and I don't care for Vimto
(though possibly you do).

Don't veto my vino!
I'm vexed past describing
when you put an embargo
on what I'm imbibing,
but I'm optimally placed
when embroiled and encased
in the ambit of cider's pure amber embrace.

I'd rather drink cider than soda or juices,
its sedulous sedative soothes and seduces,
so don't be sadistic and suddenly say
I have to drink soda, not cider, today.

INSTRUCTIONS FOR CANDIDATES

Do not turn over your paper
until instructed to do so.

You may attempt the questions in
any order you like.
You do not have to answer
in full sentences.
Some sections of the paper will be
multiple choice.

All work submitted must be
the candidate's own.
Do not write in the margins.
Write clearly and legibly
in black ink.
If you make a mistake,
draw a line through it
with a ruler
and start again.
You will not be marked on your spelling.

If there is anything you do not understand,
put your hand up
and try to attract the attention of an invigilator.
If you require any additional equipment,
put your hand up
and try to attract the attention of an invigilator.
If you feel unwell,
put your hand up
and try to attract the attention of an invigilator.

It is the candidate's own responsibility
to ensure that he or she manages the time wisely:
you will not be told how much time you have left.

When told to stop writing,
put your pen down immediately.
You must leave the examination room in silence.

The following page has been left intentionally blank.

SHOES

I   SHOES

The Marlowe boy was deemed
'a ueritable prodigie'
by the masters.
'Scholarshyppe, of course,
but bryllyaunte.'

Growing up in the town
where Becket had been filleted
for questioning a king,
he learnt by rote his *amo, amas, amat,*
already knowing his *amamus* would not be judged
the right conjugation.
He would not be taught.

They'd whitewashed over the frescos,
but he now vowed he'd paint them again
in ink.
His foul papers would be fearsome fair –
black and white, but red all over.

And Cambridge was a magic horse
and he would put his arms around its neck
and let it carry him to Parnassus.
He'd not yet learnt that there was no such place
and boys like him would never fly;
he'd always be weighed down by the ballast of his
shoes.

In the evenings, he watched his father work;
a cobbler at the last,
he hammered, stitched and buckled.

In and out it penetrates,
over and over,
an awl through the leather,
a staple through the tongue,
a poker up the arse,

a dagger through the eye.

II   APT FOR LEARNING

there will always be in our Church in Canterbury fifty poor boys, both destitute of the help of friends, and endowed with minds apt for learning, who shall be called scholars of the grammar school

Henry VIII, Statutes of Canterbury Cathedral

He was the flower of the poor boys
and they picked him,
tore him from his roots,
stuck him in a sterile vase
in an inch of water,
told him he could grow
and then made sure he couldn't,
made him thirsty,
made him thirsty,
made him thirsty,
but then wouldn't top him up.

Destitute of help,
they made him destitute of friends;
his inflation
devalued his family's currency.
His school desk became a bureau
de change, cambio, Wechsel,
where he turned himself into a noble,
a half-crown, a quarter-angel,
but the coinage was counterfeit;
he was accepted nowhere.
He no longer belonged
with farthings and groats –
they seemed to him debased –
but he would never be banked
with ducats and marks.

They said that he was well endowed
with a mind apt for learning,
but they castrated him,

turned him into a monk,
turned him into a monk,
turned him into a monk,
a churchman, a novice priest.
No plans for what they'd do with clever boys
who couldn't be penned in by a pulpit,
whose lust for knowledge ran to something other than
the Woman Taken in Adultery,
the Scarlet Whore of Babylon,
the Wedding in Cana.

III   MONSTRUOUS OPINIONS

*toching marlowes monstruous opinions [...] I cannot but
with an agreved conscience think on him or them [...] which
he would so sodenlie take slight occasion to slyp out*

Thomas Kyd

He went at God with a hot poker,
making him take it up the arse.
Iconoclast, ripping off the Elastoplast
humanity used to cover its sores,
his language was salty and he rubbed it in.
He pissed all over the sixteenth century
with his monstrous opinions,
monstrous opinions,
obnoxious positions,
refusing the pinions
of unbending gods
and their preposterous minions
in his Song of Songs:

Moses was naught but a con artist, a charlatan, a conjuror –
sing abracadabra! – elaborate hoaxer,
a decorative coaster for fragile mugs,
a cowardly chicken in a basket
found in the rushes, in denial,
a juggler without much in the way of balls.

Roll up! Roll up!
Find Our Lady in her cups,
turning tricks for centurions on street corners,
playing the virginals, unconvincingly,
practised in fingering.

The Trinity itself a three-card trick,
a badly painted triptych, squatting in two dimensions with no
perspective,
Jesus an underwhelming ta-da moment,
fake diamond, sacred heart, private members' club,

spayed, a white rabbit pulled from a hat
and on the eighth day, God said,
'I am a jealous God, a bunny boiler.'
Demanding boys be served to him tied up on altars,
nailing them spreadeagled on crosses,
ruling them with his iron sceptre.
A syphilitic, filthy old man with a fiery pillar,
a leprous third arm, a serpent that hardens to a rod
in his burning bush, a bush with a ram in it,
surprising innocents in the wilderness,
a wonky wand firing off puffs of black smoke. Our Father,
which art in heaven, harrowing be his name,
forcing our daily bread on us, prising open reluctant lips
so we can suck it and see his kingdom come.

I leave you to judge what Kit was trying to drown out
with his lushness, his loucheness, his lewdness, his loudness,
self-medicating with tobacco and boys.

IV   INTERIOR DECORATING

Marlowe could have been racked and hanged for sodomy,
deflowered by an iron maiden, had his nuts crushed in a vice
    for his 'vice'.
Today we have more humane ways to neuter gays:
vetting them like exotic pets, insisting they all love
shopping and musicals and interior decorating.
Cushioning the blow (I swear they all love choosing cushions),
softly, softly, stuffing them with soft furnishings,
upholstery, to protect us from the hard erections beneath.

Marlowe would not be stuffed.
He'd have loved to decorate your interior,
but he wasn't interested in wallpaper.
Handy with a screwdriver, a poniard, a pen,
he was no woman's best friend.
He ripped out the rhyming couplets of contemporary design,
like a naff avocado or cobalt bathroom suite,
belching lead pipes, a knackered old boiler,
replaced them with understated white verse, clean lines,
smooth plumbing, pulsing pentameter,
its beat the rise and fall of human breath,
it penetrates your eardrum, then your veins,
propels the bloody message to your heart.

LOVE

TALES OF THE UNEXPECTED

'It will happen when you least expect it' –
that's what people have been telling me since I was sixteen.
I lie in bed at night thinking about all the times and places
when I wouldn't expect it to happen.

Maybe it will happen on a train?
When the ticket inspector says, 'Single?'
he won't just be asking about my travel documentation.

Maybe it will happen at the supermarket?
When the man behind the checkout says,
'Would you like any help with your packing?'
it will be obvious exactly whose slot
he wants me to put my green tokens into.

Maybe it will happen at work?
Although hopefully not at my current work,
because that would incur a maximum seven-year prison sentence
and I'd be barred from teaching for life.

Maybe it will happen in the middle of the night?
A burglar will break in and our eyes will meet
through the hole in his balaclava and
We'll Just Know.

Maybe it will happen when I'm on the toilet?
The Man from Atlantis will swim his way up
past the U bend and surprise me
from below, or someone will ooze his way in
in aerosol form through my shower head, like frigging Zeus.

Maybe it will happen at my funeral?
There'll be an unexpectedly enterprising necrophiliac
in the congregation (also vindicating
that other staggeringly unhelpful piece of advice:
'It's never too late – it's not a race, you know.')

But, then again, maybe where I've gone wrong is in
imagining all these 'unexpected' scenarios,
so now I'm expecting them,
which is why it hasn't happened yet.

THE CLASS WAR

to John Osborne and DH Lawrence
was a vaguely homoerotic labourer
biceps globed like beef tomatoes
in a Stanley Kowalski wife-beater
taking hoity-toity posh totty
roughly from behind, laying claim
like a cat pissing in the back porch

to me, it's men who don't want me
in tweed jackets, marshmallow-soft
candy-coloured Jermyn Street shirts
with cufflinks, writing charming notes they don't mean
with a fountain pen on heavyweight paper
the nib glides with the ease of honey
falling off a silver spoon, of doors
silently opening on well-oiled hinges
and when they talk their musk-scented
burgundy-coloured vowels, rounded at the edges
like a well-sucked cough sweet, have the unfakeable
centuries-old patina of a Queen Anne table
handed down through the family, part of their background
for so long, they don't even see it

JESUS WANTED ME FOR A SUNBEAM

Jesus wanted me for a sunbeam,
or so I was told.
I was that long-lost sheep
He wanted in his fold.

No, don't mock!
When he came to knock,
I joined the flock.
They said that he would dock
my tail and shear my fleece,
and I said, 'Yes, please!'
because I longed for that perfect peace
that they talked about.

But I didn't find peace in the house of the Lord
and blessings were not poured
out on me.
For, behold, a man came from heaven
(or, at any rate, from a neighbouring church)
and he said, 'Take, eat, this is my body.'

Some long-buried earthly sense told me that I should refuse,
that this was a ruse,
that he was bad news.

But they taught me to look for miracles
and I thought it was a sign
that every time he touched me
my water turned to wine
and I was a foolish virgin –
it was dark and I was damp –
so I let him dip his wick
and burn the oil in my lamp,
the extra virgin olive oil
in its tightly stoppered drum
I was saving for the bridegroom,
but the bridegroom had not come.

Together we worked wonders:
he broke my bread, I shared his fishes.
He reached my land of milk and honey
and he said it was delicious.
He found the light beneath my bushel
and he saw that it was nice.
He split my oyster, then he found
my pearl beyond all price
and I thought the eye of his needle was
my gate to Paradise.

But afterwards, he always said,
'Let's keep this to ourselves for a bit.
Don't tell anyone – it
can be our little secret.'

And there was more –
he took grave exception
to contraception;
he condemned condoms,
pilloried the Pill.
'What we did in bed
was sinful,' he said,
but the sin was enhanced
if planned in advance –
his answer was banning
family planning.

And I spent weeks
waiting anxiously to bleed,
then he'd
fume and he'd flap,
say I was trying to trap
him. His life would be defiled
if I had his child.

And for a while
I was in denial
until one day at work
I helped a mate
moving heavy furniture.
That night, as I bled a river
of thick black clots,
I looked at the date
and said, 'It's just my period –
three months late.'

Then one day
we were at a bar
and he handed me a chalice
and said, 'Take, drink, this is my blood.'
But it was not blood.
And it was not just wine.
It knocked me out as cold as Lazarus
and when I came to in my bed,
I didn't remember getting home.
And I tried to rise again,
but his body was pinning me down
like a stone I couldn't roll away.

I'd asked for an egg
and he gave me a scorpion,
I'd asked for a fish
and he gave me a snake,
so I cried to the Church
and said, 'Someone, please help me!
Please help me, someone,
for Jesus's sake.'

And they said, 'Judge not,
that ye be not judged.
We cannot cast a stone.
No one can condemn his sin

but Jesus Christ alone.
We have to show forgiveness
no matter what he's done.'
He was the late-hired vineyard worker,
he was the prodigal fucking son,
he was the wicked tax collector
who atoned and climbed a tree,
so they killed the fatted calf for him
and they crucified me.

STRIPPED

I practised saying the words aloud
in my room, loving how they felt in my mouth.
I was a child wearing her first pair
of shiny real grown-up shoes
wanting to wear them in bed, in the bath,
breaking them in.

At work, I ached for my colleagues to say,
'Doing anything this weekend?'
so I could casually reply, 'Nothing much.
Just chilling with my boyfriend.
My boyfriend and I will probably go for a drink
at my boyfriend's favourite pub,
then I might go back to my boyfriend's house
and spend the night. You know, with my boyfriend.'

I felt like a Brownie who had finally gained a badge
after years of trying, her 'Being Normal' badge,
and she might have been the last one in the pack to get it,
but she was damn well going to sew it on her uniform.

I wanted to put it on my CV. Other achievements:
directing a play at the Edinburgh Fringe,
basic conversational Polish and
having a boyfriend.

People often say, 'I don't understand
why women stay in abusive relationships.
They must be fucking stupid.
Surely they've got no one to blame
but themselves?'

Well, I understand. I still hate the people who 'rescued' me,
overofficious Health and Safety meddlers,
confiscating my lifeboat because it was faulty,
but not replacing it with one that was watertight:
just dropped me back into the cold, vast sea.

They stripped me of my Olympic medal,
made time run backwards,
recorded over my mixtape of love songs.
They didn't just end what I thought I had –
they unbegan it.

MISTAKEN IDENTITY

That sepia-saffron, sunwashed day
we went to Turville in the car,
like drunkards thinking they can walk straight,
we thought the others hadn't noticed we were
still fuzzy with fucking
and, with nods and grins,
we were wildly semaphoring to each other
private jokes that were
all too public.
There was a Norman church there
and you blah-blah-blahed a lot
about ancestors buried there
(only you could namedrop in a graveyard,
my plummy-vowelled, pink-shirted, pedigree chum!).
Then I raced you up the hill,
thinking the others hadn't noticed
my eyes were on your body in motion
and the snail tracks of sweat
in the V of your shirt.
And we saw a red kite,
but you insisted it was a golden eagle.
You traced its wheeling and soaring through the sky,
whooping and laughing,
and I traced your wheeling and soaring,
whooping and laughing,
because, at that point, I still thought you
were a golden eagle
and was yet to be disabused.

LASHINGS

I am tired of this subterfuge.
Oh, at first, it was very exciting,
like Enid Blyton – having a password
for our gang, the Secret Two.

Hunkering down in our garden shed
with chocolate biscuits and home-brewed ginger beer,
building up a storm of gas beneath its cork,
dangerously effervescent and spicy.

The hints you dropped in public!
In plain sight, like letters written
in lemon juice that I had to hold over
the flame of our shared past to be able to read!

Much more interesting than what the adults do,
fidelity a weak and tepid cup of tea
they drink out of habit, or to prove
that they're grown-up (which I decline to be).

But now I want to be something more substantial
than your imaginary friend. I want you to be more than
a fictional character in an adventure novel I read
under the bedclothes, with a torch, when everyone's asleep.

I feel as real as a stick woman chalked on a pavement
just before a cloudburst and I need you to tag me
so people know I'm It. But 'love' is the word
we can't say out loud, or we'll both be
out.

TREATWISE

'Don't make yourself cheap.'

                'Always let the man do the running.'

'Remember – you're the prize.'

            'Men prefer a challenge.'

'Cultivate an air of mystery.'

     'If he's attractive, it probably means he's a bastard.
          Best stick with the ugly ones.
          You know they genuinely care.'

'It's not very ladylike.'

          'Do you want him to think you're desperate?'

'Do you want him to think you're a tart?'

       'No! Why did you phone him?
You're always supposed to let the man phone first!'

'Can't you just give him a chance?'

                  'He's a good man.'

'He really likes you.'

            'You'll hurt his feelings!'

'Don't be shallow!'

      'Don't be cruel!'

           'Don't be picky!'

'You ought to be flattered!'

'You ought to be grateful!'

'At your age, you've got to take what you can get.'

I'm not going to swallow it any longer –
the You'll-Get-What-You're-Given,
Eat-Up-Your-Greens-Don't-You-Know-People-In-Africa-Are-
    Starving life that all women are inducted into.

I want the chocolate torte,
not the bread-and-butter pudding!
I want to have a look at the à la carte menu.
If the dish I want is out of my price range or sold out –
fine. I'm not going to force my way into the kitchen
and strongarm the chef. I'll just pick something else.
But let me choose.

I'm no longer going to take the toffee penny
because someone else might want the strawberry creme.

I'm going to lick melted butter from my fingers,
suck all the jam out of the doughnut,
eat the pizza topping and leave the crust.
I'm going to eat Coco Pops for dinner,
have my pudding before my main course.
I don't give a fuck what the UK Chief Medical Officer
recommends.

I'm not going to be fobbed off
with the fat-free, no-added-sugar alternative.
I'm afraid I'm going to be very naughty.
I'm not going to eat my vegetables.
You can't make me.

Please, sir – can I have some more?

EVERYTHING REMINDS ME OF YOU

Everything reminds me of you.
No! I mean *everything* reminds me of you.

There's this performance poet
who was the warm-up act
to a more famous performance poet
at a gig I was at, and,
without my glasses,
he reminded me of you.
But then I saw him again
when I did have my glasses
and I realised that
actually
the only real point of resemblance
is that you're both vaguely blond
and it made me want to smash my glasses,
so then all vaguely blond men
would look like you.

The equal opportunities monitoring form
that came with the job application
I just filled in –
that reminded me of you:
as I ticked 'White British',
my eyes were, naturally, drawn
to the other options
further down the page
and they fixed on one, as I thought to myself,
'That's your ethnicity!'

And I know I'll probably never get the job
and be stuck on Jobseekers' fucking Allowance
for the rest of my natural life,
but it doesn't matter,
because I know that I have touched
a piece of paper
in a drawer

in a filing cabinet
in the office of a human resources department somewhere
(which, according to their data protection policy,
they may keep for up to five years!)
which mentions your ethnicity.

And, on the, sadly, extremely rare occasions
that you favourite one of my tweets on Twitter,
I love the way that the notifications
that pop up in my e-mail
have your name on them.
You've found your way into my inbox,
which, come to think of it,
sounds like it ought to be
some kind of sexual euphemism
and, God, I wish it was!

And I looked your name up
on one of those baby name websites
and it turns out it means
the exact same thing in Sanskrit
that my name means in Greek,
so now even my own name reminds me of you,
which is a bit unfortunate,
as now, every time someone calls me,
instead of answering them,
I just sit there staring wistfully into the middle distance
with a little streak of dribble running down my chin.

And I know I'm old enough to be your mother
and I know you've already got a girlfriend
and you're an uber-hottie and I'm a bit of a minger
and if you ever heard this poem
and realised it was about you,
well, you'd probably take out a restraining order…

…but then there'd be a restraining order

with both our names on it!
And a restraining order is a legal document, right?
Well, so is a marriage certificate!
So it would be a bit like us getting married,
but just not quite.

CROSS

Red Man looks tense,
squaring up to the pedestrian,
shoulders hunched, elbows crooked,
feet spread to lower his centre of gravity,
a nightclub bouncer expecting trouble,
fingers almost on his hips
like he's patting his pockets for a cigarette
or just didn't know what to do with his hands.
He's clearly got issues and probably a prison record,
maybe not a candidate for Mensa, but
I kind of think I'd like him
as a colleague or a neighbour.
What you saw would be what you got.

Green Man fancies himself something rotten.
The way he flips his right hand looks a little camp,
but you can tell by the length of his stride
and the casually expansive arm gestures
he's got a straight man's sense of entitlement,
thinks he owns that road,
a charming psychopath or poisonously passive-aggressive.
He'd speak in heightened RP and your mother would adore
him.
He'd insist on ordering the pizza in Italian to impress you,
send you statement flowers via Interflora,
then fuck your best friend behind your back.

AFTER LARKIN

The vast, warm store on the high street,
pimping overpriced clothes. An overheated house
of mandatory fun, where placards
shriek, 'Mix It Up!' 'Playful Colours!'
above rails of sour lemons, hard emeralds, thorned roses,
chains, belts, clutches, tights, corsets,
wire cages trimmed with lace, deceitful
whites that you know will renege
to grey within a couple of washes,
where uniforms with clipboards
guard a chilly hall of mirrors.
They tag you with a number, before
hiding you behind a heavy curtain.

But past the columns of structured separates,
past the headless mannequins twisted
into seductive poses, past a line of twill slacks
pressed into knife pleats confronting you,
a flight of airforce blue, a whole flotilla of navies,
sprawl Men's Casuals. Charcoal that glows
into umber, groves of olive, a Sahara
of khaki opens out before you. Airy
boxers flap in the breeze from the fan,
elasticated slips bunch on a pair of thrusting hips,
Y-fronts, algebraic in their mysteries, enfold
a value you'll never find, an insoluble equation

that warns us we will never know what men are,
or what they do, that they will always lounge
beyond the limits of our striplit section,
loose-knit, light jersey leisurewear
printed with cartoon characters.

LOVE IS A REALLY DIFFICULT FOREIGN LANGUAGE

Love is a really difficult foreign language
I never learnt at school –
only the top set got to do it
while I got packed off to extra piano practice, instead.

I sometimes listened in
when my classmates were doing their homework,
but I only got confused –
so many rules to remember,
everything had to be modified according to gender
and it seemed impossibly hard
to change a singular into a plural.

But in my gap year I travelled
and gained a smattering –
mostly learning the several hundred words
they have for 'goodbye'.

By the end of university,
those who'd majored in it had charged so far ahead –
graduated from the simple present to the future perfect,
while I couldn't seem to move on from the past continuous –
I knew I'd never catch them up.

I haven't bothered keeping it up since.

People tell me it's not too late –
I could pick it up at night school
or find a course online –

but I'd rather shout in English,
make hand gestures,
than try to speak Love brokenly
and know I'll never be fluent,

a clumsy false beginner

practising basic conjugation
with others equally inept
organised by the teacher
into arbitrary pairs,

mechanically asking each other,
'Have you got the time?'
or 'Would you like to see a film?'
when it's obviously only a rote-learnt
skills-building exercise
and we don't really want to know,

honking nasally,
our thick tongues and slow lips
fumbling and mangling what ought to be musical,
always laboriously constructing,
always putting our endings in the wrong place.

Sometimes, though, I eavesdrop on native speakers,
not understanding,
feeling foreign
but envying the way it comes to them like breathing,
wanting to converse with them,
knowing I never will.

REJECTION IN THE AGE OF TWITTER

Bovver-boot-bruised, your heart winces;
you've been given a good kicking
with your own unanswered DMs.

You've conditioned yourself to salivate
at the sight of the bell icon,
yet, unaddressed, unfranked,
the grey envelope never turns blue,
a litmus test he's failed, but,
reluctant to accept the results,
you enter him for endless resits.

That blue bird promised to take your heart
on a water-speed-record-breaking ride,
but your target was too ambitious;
flipped over and smashed,
your hopes now lie submerged
in a cold, cold lake.

And you know you ought to put yourself on mute,
untag him, unfollow, but how can you when, at your age,
all the unattached men in the whole world worth having
form a dramatis personae limited to fewer than 140 characters?

TOWN PLANNING

They built the church where my sister got married
twenty-five years ago on a hillside,
so its spire could give me the finger
everywhere I go in this town,
pointing to everything I've failed to do and am not,
a sky-sized sheet of inadequacies,
and I can't block it out.
It's always there, fucking up my horizon.

And I'm locked out of those ecru terraces,
houses knitted together in a regular pattern,
tight ribbing, cable stitch,
their gardens with trampolines and tricycles,
barbecue sets, extra-large bins for the nappies,
brick patios, Flymos, overcomplicated flower beds,
places I wouldn't want to live,
their upkeep beyond me,
but I still feel snubbed by their hedges,
by the smug, show-off security
that plunges me in the limelight
when I walk past at night.
I've seen my reflection in the window of their people-carrier
and it's not nice.

THE GUARDIANS

I use the names of people I love,
people who were once briefly kind to me,
as passwords, talismans I touch
several times a day, my fingers

seeking out their gentle kiss in the keys
to my treasure chest, my word hoard.
They stand sentry, ward off harm.
I type and, by the magic of megabytes,
they are transfigured into little stars.

I wish upon them.

LIKE

I've never had much luck with men,
not had the love life I deserved.
It doesn't help that I'm like a library copy of the latest novel by
    JK Rowling, writing as Robert Galbraith:
always reserved.

I can't give off flirty signals.
I'm very shy indeed.
I'm like the end credits of a Sunday-night BBC drama:
very hard to read.

And some men get scared by my intelligence –
they don't like it when I say things they don't understand
and it makes them feel like Bridgwater Station between the
    hours of 2.30pm and midnight, Monday to Saturday and
    all day Sunday:
unmanned.

The kind of males that chat me up
just don't appeal to me –
maybe because most of them are like the recommended
    ambient centigrade temperature for the safe storage of
    foods:
under eight, or over sixty-three.

While when men my own age chat me up,
the prospects still aren't bright,
because, for some indefinable reason I can't quite put
    my finger on, they're like the dominant hand of Paul
    McCartney, John McEnroe and Osama bin Laden:
not right.

My friends tried to set me up with a man.
They thought we'd make the perfect pair,
but it was like my school timetable, once I'd finally made it
    into the sixth form and could drop all the subjects I was
    shit at:
there was absolutely no chemistry there.

And when I do meet a man who lights my fire,
who makes my heartrate surge and my nipples tingle,
he's like the finest cream in the chiller cabinet at Asda:
not single.

I cannot find a boyfriend,
despite my best endeavour.
I'm like the MMR vaccine and autism:
no relationship, whatsoever.

So, while I have the attention
of all you lovely people here,
like a person who's just enrolled on a glass-blowing course,
I want to make something clear:

Platonically, I'm sorted.
I've got lots of lovely mates,
but, like someone shopping for their Christmas cake
ingredients,
I'm looking for dates.

I'll shut up on this subject now,
but let me leave you in no doubt.
I am not like the books in the reference section of Bristol
    Central Library:
you can take me out.

POLAND

SMAK

That first night in Łódź, I lost my appetite.
I'd picked up some basics in a Stalinist minimart
that smelt like a pet shop,
appalled by the horror film specimens
suspended in jars on the shelves
and the barrel by the counter where fungal buboes
bobbed in vinegar
yet figuring I couldn't go wrong
with bread and bottled water,
but back in my room
the water tasted of the fume cupboard
in my school chemistry lab,
the bread was a rancid rye sourdough,
grey as a pair of pilling pants,
when an English loaf was a clean and safe
polythene-wrapped bath sponge.

In the weeks that followed, I lost weight, despaired
of finding foods uncontaminated with plum jam
the colour and texture of earwax,
the rising-damp, sink-trap flavour of dill.
Everything was booby-trapped;
even the fluffy cream filling of a cake
leaked the urinal tang of vodka. It all tasted dirty. Carnal,
like honey or sweat or semen.

British food was printed in block colours,
outlined in a black felt tip,
but in Poland tastes smudged and slurred, hazy watercolours.
Smoky, adult,
like a bending note on a saxophone, a gasp, a moan, an ache,
like the nasal vowels in *pączki, wędliny, gołąbki,
mężczyzna.* I grew to like it.

MARS

I want a snack. It's winter, it's minus fifteen degrees
and all that snow is making me hungry.
I only have ten minutes before I have to teach my class,
so I stop off at that shop at the top of Piotrkowska,
the main street. It's the shop with the orange door.
I don't normally go in there – it's expensive
and doesn't sell a lot except hard liquor,
but it does sell chocolate. There's a display on the counter
of Western chocolate bars – Mars, Snickers, Bounty, Milky Way.
The only other customers in there
are an old lady with a hat that looks like a tea cosy
and hair that hasn't been washed or brushed for so long
that it's turned into felt, a man with a wispy beard
and long flowing clothes who looks like Dumbledore
and who's muttering to himself, and a guy who smells of meths
who's got a badly-trained Rottweiler on a fraying lead.
I go up to the counter,
the assistant smiles at me and asks what I want
and I point at one of the bars and say,
'*Baton* Mars, *poproszę*,' and by the time
I've got to the end of the first word
she's stopped smiling and I can see
she's clocked from my accent that I'm foreign.

When I first moved here, it wouldn't have taken her that long.
People knew just from looking at me not to ask me for directions,
but sometimes they'd shout stuff for a laugh, like,
'Chapter 1, Exercise 1: listen and repeat.
Do you come from Manchester? No, I come from Warsaw.'
But I've lived here for three years now. I've gone native.
I'm wearing Polish-made clothes, I've adopted Polish posture,
I've even got Polish-coloured hair.
You wouldn't know I wasn't born here
until I open my mouth, which I just have,
and she's shrugging and saying, '*Nie rozumiem*' –
'I don't understand.'

Now, I'll be the first to admit that I can't say my 'r's properly
even in English, and Polish is a rhotic language.
I said 'Mars', when they would say 'Marrrs'.
That's like saying 'bar' to an English person when you meant
        'bra'
or 'gay' when you meant 'grey'
('That man is very old, so his hair has gone gay') –
you sound a bit like a two-year-old,
but it's usually perfectly clear from the context what you mean,
especially if you are pointing at a Mars bar in a display cabinet
where there are literally only four or five other options.

But I give her the benefit of the doubt and try again, anyway,
this time enunciating as clearly as I possibly can:
'*Baton*' – bar, 'Mars' – Mars, '*poproszę*' – please.
She laughs and shrugs and keeps telling me
she doesn't understand,
and I can understand every single word of Polish she's speaking,
but she apparently doesn't understand me.
And I'm getting worried about being late for my class,
so I start circumlocuting desperately,
in an attempt to make myself clear:
'*Baton czekoladowy angielski z karmelem
w opakowaniu czerwono-czarnym.
Tamten pomiędzy* Bounty *i* Snickers.'
It's like playing Pictionary.

But she's still smirking and shrugging
and now she's trying to bring the guy
who smells of meths with the badly-trained Rottweiler on a
        fraying lead
into it, catching his eye and shrugging,
as if to say, 'Bloody foreigners, eh?'
and doing the internationally recognised symbol for 'idiot'.
But the guy who smells of meths
and has a badly-trained Rottweiler on a fraying lead
isn't having any of it and he's getting really angry on my behalf.

He catches my eye and shrugs, as if to say,
'Bloody xenophobes, eh?' and he barks at her,
'*Ona chciałabym* Mars,' and soon the woman
wearing a tea cosy and with hair like felt is joining in,
'*Daj jej czekoladę,*' and then the man
who looks like Dumbledore and is muttering to himself
is on board, as well, and they're all shouting at her in unison,
'Just give her a fucking Mars bar!'
and in the end she has to serve me,
even though she doesn't want to,
and I say, '*Dziękuję bardzo,*' to the other people in the shop
and they nod back pleasantly, and on my way out
the guy who smells of meths with a badly-trained Rottweiler
    on a fraying lead
shakes my hand.

I thought about this incident in the run-up to the Brexit vote,
when Boris Johnson and Michael Gove
were the ones behind the counter,
wearing a nylon overall,
faking a smile and saying, 'Hello. I'm your server for today.
How may I help?' and EU citizens were saying,
'I don't want to be separated from my family,'
and asylum seekers were saying,
'I don't want to be sent back to certain death,'
and the *Windrush* generation were saying,
'I want to stay in my home, where I have a legal right to be,
and not be sent back to a country I don't even remember,'
and Boris and Michael pretended they couldn't understand
and shrugged and smirked, as if to say, 'Bloody foreigners,
eh?'
I thought the British public
would be like the other people in the queue
and refuse to play along. But we didn't.
We behaved with less intelligence and decency
than a guy who smelt of meths with a badly-trained Rottweiler
    on a fraying lead.

INTERMEDIATE POLISH

Today I am revising the formal 'you'
in a land where strangers are always chaperoned
by the third person,
where subject and object are clearly marked
and gender changes
everything.
For centuries, the passive voice of Europe,
muted by invasion, occupation.
The tyrants treated them like dogs,
whipped their children for speaking Polish in the schools,
forced them to bark in German, whine in Russian.
At night, in their kennels, tails between their legs,
they gnawed on the bones of their language:
its grammar.

Acting as a collective noun, they agreed
they'd not forget the name of any person, place or thing;
they'd predicate rebellion on syntactic lines,
make every verb a 'doing' word.
Too frail to take up arms, too proud to flee,
they challenged their oppressors in the only way they could:
they stuck their tongue out at them.
That's why their speech is olde worlde, starched, correct,
a tablecloth that Grandma folded, put away and kept for best.
While other nations slouch in denim, have dropped inflections
like a hamburger wrapper in the street,
their language still conjugates and declines
with the couples ballroom dancing in the nightclubs,
moustachioed young men who bend at the waist
to kiss your hand,
purple-haired ladies patronising
tobacco-coloured shops
selling nothing but lace curtains.

THE BATTENBERG REPUBLIC

Twenty years back in England,
I still live partly on the Continent.
I drink my coffee treacle-strong and from a glass.
The cheese sandwich seems to me to be
the ideal breakfast food.
Some words still come to me
in Polish first, mostly private, household things:
I clean my carpets with an *odkurzacz*,
unblock my drains with *kret*.
My English is wound round with Slavic circumlocutions:
coffee without caffeine,
liquid for the washing of dishes, grated roll,
not without danger.

Those first days back after four years away, England
concussed me. The lights in the supermarket were
too bright, the choice too much.
I kept getting into the wrong side of cars,
offering sweets to strangers on trains,
knocking on toilet cubicle doors to see if they were vacant,
spoke my own language with a foreign accent.

We expats used to joke about a nation we would found,
the Battenberg Republic, its flag chequered pink and yellow,
a nation for people who don't like their own country much
but never feel fully at home anywhere else,
a country where you needn't choose
between strawberry and almond –
you can have your cake and eat it,
where identity is as mouldable as marzipan
and the gaps are filled with jam.

LIFE

MENTAL

Good evening. This is your captain speaking.
This is not, as you may have been expecting,
an ATOL-protected package tour of Bedlam
where you get to feel heartwarmingly sorry
for the mad people
from behind the reinforced Perspex
of your own privilege.

Because poems like that drive me mental
and, trust me, I was already mental enough.

No, I am a suicide bomber
who has hijacked your plane
and is set to fly it, all engines blazing,
straight into the centre of the mess that is my head.

I have thrown out countless cups of tea
because I suddenly see a bottle of bleach
on the counter and,
although it's on the other side of the kitchen,
it sets off a metonymic frenzy in my head:

Bleach, tea,
bleach, tea,
bleach, tea.
Teach. Blea.
There's bleach in the tea!
There's bleach in the tea!
And I swear I can actually taste the chlorine
burning my gullet.
So I'll drink eight pints of water
to dilute the chemicals
that aren't in my stomach,
then stay up 'til four o'clock in the morning
looking up
water poisoning on the internet.

I once watched an episode
of *Midsomer Murders*
where I was following a totally different plot
from everybody else, because, at one point,
Inspector Barnaby opened the lid of his dustbin,
then got into the car
WITHOUT WASHING HIS HANDS FIRST.
I watched in horror as he smeared toxic germs
on the door handle, the hand brake, the steering wheel.
Then he got out a bag of sweets and handed one to Troy,
who took it. And so the contagion spread.
There was nothing I could do as they gleefully
contaminated Midsomer Barton, Midsomer Priors
and the whole of Causton CID.

While all the other viewers
were wondering if it was Colonel Blimp
in the library with the lead piping
or Mrs Cook in the kitchen with the rope
I knew it was John Nettles with the biological warfare
absolutely bloody everywhere.

Obsessive thoughts are a bit like
when a really tall, fat person
sits in front of you in the cinema.
You think it's going to be all right,
that you can see round him,
but when you crane in one direction
he always seems to move, too,
and you miss all the best bits of the film,
because his head is always in the fucking way.

Well, I'm missing the best bits of this film,
because my own head is always in the way.

THE ARTISTS' EXPRESS

Welcome aboard the Artists' Express –
a non-stop shuttle service
between Delusional Overconfidence and Total Self-Loathing.
This train will not be calling at Healthy Confidence,
Realistic Self-Appraisal, Mild Doubt
or Constructive Goalsetting.

Please take a moment to familiarise yourself
with the safety instructions
on the card on the back of the seat in front of you,
so you can completely ignore them. You're an artist.
We live dangerously.

The buffet car is situated between coaches D and E,
currently open and serving
a piece of cake, a bowl of cherries,
pie in the sky made with puff pastry,
melting moments,
custard with a very thin skin,
rocky road, hard cheese, crumble,
bitter lemon, sour grapes.

Do not leave your baggage unattended at any time.
Instead, please ensure all the other passengers are fully aware
of exactly how much baggage you have.
Have a poke around in it.
Find all your dirty linen and put it on display.

If you notice anyone on the train acting suspiciously,
don't worry about it. It's probably one of our regulars.
They're all like that.

Ticket inspectors will be making regular patrols,
just to make you really paranoid
that you might not have a valid ticket for the Artists' Express
and don't really deserve to be here.

When we reach the outskirts of Total Self-Loathing
this service will experience a lengthy delay,
as we make way for the fast-track Career Express
from Humble Beginnings to Fabulous Success Beyond Your
      Wildest Dreams.
At this point, we will pull into a siding
for approximately twenty years,
to allow everybody you have ever spoken to
in your entire life to overtake you.

Please mind the gap
between your aspirations
and your actual level of achievement.
Mind it.
Really, really mind it.

On alighting the train, please ensure
you have all your personal belongings with you.
Please also ensure you don't use words like 'alighting'
in your work – it will really piss editors off.
And 'personal belongings' is tautology,
which isn't great, either.
But you know you're never going to get off this train, right?
Because if you did, you wouldn't be an artist.

SLAM-WINNING POEM

I've been trying to write a slam-winning poem,
a poem that will make people cry.
Are you working on a tear-jerking, searching,
plain-speaking, attention-seeking, curiosity-piquing piece
about how you were in pieces?
Up to your neck in elephant faeces?
Have you been using up whole bottles of ink
writing about how you were on the brink
and you nearly killed yourself?

Yeah, well, I can go one better than that,
because I ALWAYS CAN!
I actually *did* kill myself.
Twice.
Because this is a slam-winning poem:
bigger, better, sadder than yours.
In the sob-story, misery-memoir nuclear arms race,
I've got the biggest warhead,
packed with more enriched bluetonium
than a Christmas episode of *EastEnders*
guest-scripted by Leonard Cohen and Morrissey.

Lack of issues? Not going to be an issue,
because my poem is raising awareness of the plight
of underprivileged black and Asian polar bears
with Ebola,
shivering on their tiny, fractured islands
as the Arctic ice cap melts, eroded
by the capitalist machinations
of the homophobic patriarchy.
My poem is going to state the fucking obvious,
several times.
Murder is really bad.
When murder happens, people get killed,
which means they die,
and this makes their loved ones very sad.
Because there's nothing

94

a spoken word audience can get behind
like something which has already been said
a million times before
much better by someone else
and which no one except a psychopath
could possibly disagree with.

Sexism is bad, racism is bad... ooh!
I haven't done a rap yet.
But, then again, there are some things
which a post-menopausal woman should never attempt,
like Olympic-standard gymnastics
or using textspeak non-ironically.
But I *can* put *on* that *strange* iambic voice,
do that *thing* with my *arm* where it *looks*
like I'm *taking* my *cycling* proficiency *test*.
And PUT an emphasis on random WORDS
as I build to a schmaltzy crescendo.
Give me a ten! Give me a ten!
Give me a T! Give me an E! Give me an N!

Because this, ladies and gentlemen,
is a slam-winning poem!

MY CHRISTMAS TREE WAS MANUFACTURED IN THE PEOPLE'S REPUBLIC OF CHINA

It is essentially a collection
of bottle-green bottle brushes
stuck at random angles
to a plastic base.

My Christmas tree was manufactured
in the People's Republic of China.
It's a Yuletide monstrosity, I'm sure you'll agree.
Hope you're not very in the mood
for verisimilitude,
as it's not very similar to any tree.

Its resemblance to a spruce
is pretty loose.
If you asked me, 'Does it look like a fir?'
I'd have to demur.
And it's not much like a pine
in its design.

My Christmas tree was manufactured
in the People's Republic of China.
It's an arboreal memorial of all that is rank;
its plasticky bulk is so hard to manoeuvre,
its dendriform dandruff's a bugger to hoover
and it's lost more branches than the NatWest bank.

My Christmas tree was manufactured
in the People's Republic of China.
It's sadly symbolic of my life's empty cup:
it's moulting like mad,
it looks shabby and sad
and I can't even remember when I last had it up.

My Christmas tree was manufactured
in the People's Republic of China,

a provenance which may seem slightly wrong to us,
when 'Hark! The Herald Angels Sing'
and Chairman Mao and Deng Xiaoping
are things which seem a little bit incongruous.

Or are they?

Because think about it for a minute:
robin redbreast, red poinsettia,
red-suited Santa, the holly bears a berry
as red as any blood,
Red Square, red star, Red Army,
reds under the beds…
I think you can see where I'm going with this:
according to Donald Trump logic,
an alarming proportion of carol singers
have become dangerously radicalised.

My Christmas tree's a Marxist infiltrator!
Despite its festive holiday veneer,
its intentions are quite solemn:
it's an evergreen fifth column.
O, Tannenbaum! The red flag's flying here.

ACKNOWLEDGEMENTS

I am enormously grateful to the editors of the following journals, where some of these poems previously appeared, in some cases in a slightly different version:

Algebra of Owls, Amaryllis, Clear Poetry, Clockwise Cat, The Frogmore Papers, The High Window, The Interpreter's House, Obsessed with Pipework, Spilling Cocoa over Martin Amis.

'Secret Passages' was written for the show *Rational Creatures*, part of the Jane Austen Festival, Bath, 2018.

I owe a debt of gratitude to far more people than I could possibly fit on this page, but they include:

Philippa Basham, Tom Denbigh, Bev Dewey, Tom Dewey, Marilyn Edbrooke, Anna Freeman, Robert Garnham, Thommie Gillow, Alison Green, Sam Grudgings, Tim King, Damian O'Vitch, Danny Pandolfi, Casper Sare, Gina Sherman at Apples and Snakes, Hannah Teasdale, Liv Torc. Above all, to Clive Birnie, Harriet Evans, Bridget Hart and the rest of the Burning Eye team.

Lightning Source UK Ltd.
Milton Keynes UK
UKHW041520060119
335081UK00001B/61/P